UNDERSTAND
HOW TO DRAW DS4

Drawing
Figures & Portraits

George Cayford

SEARCH PRESS

Wellwood North Farm Road Tunbridge Wells

Introduction

Artists have always wanted to record what people, famous and unknown, look like. The male and female figure have represented ideals of heroism and beauty, as witness the countless drawings, paintings and sculpture handed down from the ancient Greeks to the present day. We are fascinated by our own species, and by the variety of forms and expressions the human body represents. Because individual humans are unique, there is always something new to learn as we draw or paint from each model; every pose, expression and gesture is a challenge to our skills.

In this book I will offer guidelines to help you understand the challenges and problems of people. While I hardly mention anatomy, the great study of classical artists — that is a subject for another book — my illustrations and words will describe how I approach the drawing of people and their different features and characters.

One question I am often asked is, how do you find your models? The first point to remember is that everybody is interesting to an artist who wishes to practise his or her art. I have access to models in two ways. I attend my local life class in the evening where there is almost always a professional nude model posing for the students; and I also ask people to pose for me. It is surprisingly successful if you adopt a sensible — dare I say professional — approach. My family and friends are my first source. Many people are flattered to be asked to pose for a portrait or clothed study. For nude studies a relative or friend might be prepared to pose — people nowadays are less shy of revealing their bodies than when I was a student.

You could also try forming your own life-class with a group of friends, working in one of your own homes and sharing between you the cost of having a model.

Another way of drawing from a model or models is to ask permission to take your sketchpad along to a local keep-fit class or dance studio. It will give you good practice in looking at the human form, how it articulates, its variety and shape. The members may not hold poses for very long, but quick sketches of people in motion or momentary repose can be equally satisfying, and will build up your confidence in your drawing. Swimming pools and beaches are another source. If there is a museum or gallery near you that has a collection of

classical sculpture, again, get permission to draw these, for they are models that never move. Always try to draw from the three-dimensional figure, and not from photographs or illustrations, for in this way you train your eye and hand to interpret three-dimensional form in to a two-dimensional medium.

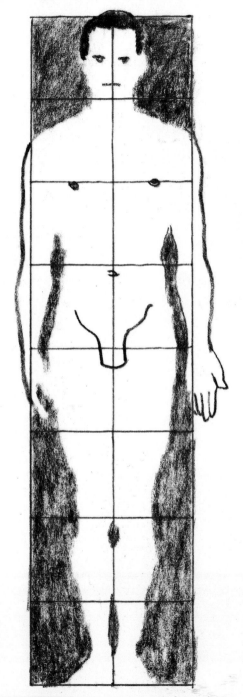

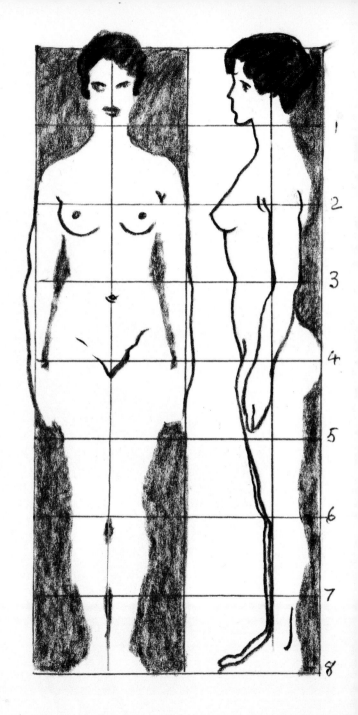

Body proportions

Before you start drawing, it is as well to understand the proportions of the human figure. The most easily learned, and the one most artists use, is to measure the body in heads. Generally speaking, the rule is that the height of an adult figure is eight times the depth of the head, or eight heads tall. From this rule the other dimensions and components of the body can be broken down into heads, arms, legs, and torso.

The rule applies to both the male and the female body, but obviously there are anatomical differences between the two. The male body is usually taller than the female. It is also wider at the shoulders and narrower across the hips than the female. In the diagram on the opposite page, I have divided a male and a female body into their respective 'heads'. You can see how the differences between the two sexes 'fit' into these divisions, or extend beyond them. If you get into the habit of assessing the models you draw by this rule of 'heads', and then adjust their individual proportions accordingly, you have a simple but effective means of drawing the human body in front of you, whether it is clothed or nude.

But people do not stand in front of you like a diagram. They shift from leg to leg, they slump or stretch, twist and turn. The spine is the main support and strength of the body, and the body articulates from it. It naturally takes on an S-curve when viewed from the side but also assumes other curves as the limbs and torso move. Look for this main curve within the torso and then articulate head, shoulder and hip angles from it. Balance, too, is important to observe. The centre of gravity shifts as the body moves about and the 'centre line' moves accordingly, usually springing from near the foot where the body's weight rests. The diagram on the right shows lines of articulation in a standing male body with the weight on the left leg.

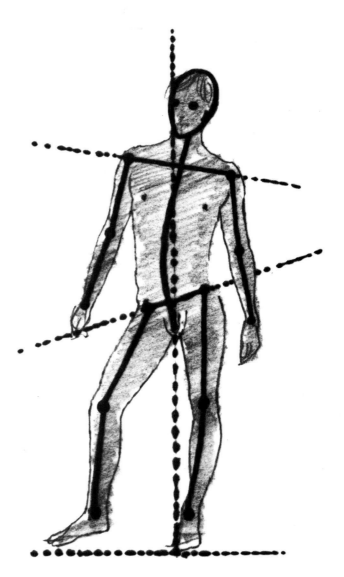

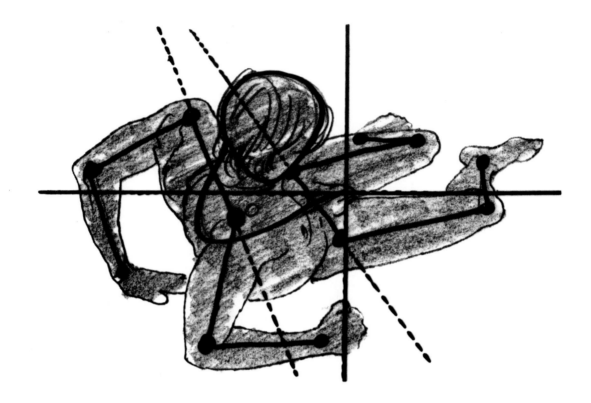

Articulation

If the spine is the indicator from which we can understand the articulation of the body, then it follows that the arms, legs and neck are extensions which interact with the spine to produce its S-curve. Our extremities also hold us up, allow us to sit or recline. The two main centres of articulation here, as we saw on page 5, are the shoulders and the hips or pelvis. Even with a seemingly complicated pose, such as the foreshortened view of a semi-reclining body in the drawing above, so long as its articulation is seen, then the pose can be drawn confidently.

Over this figure I have drawn the spinal curve from the neck to the pelvis, and across it the directions in which the shoulders and the pelvis are rotated about it. From the shoulder points and the hip points I have also drawn in the directions the limbs are articulated. Op-

posite, on page 7, are drawings of a standing male nude in different poses, with a 'stick form' drawn over them to show articulation of the main forms. Try drawing the 'stick form' first, before you actually draw your figure. Notice how I put a blob where something happens: the shoulder and hip points, ankles, knees, elbows, wrists. Even where you cannot see a part of the body, draw it in stick-fashion, as I have with the shoulders and hips of the left-hand figure.

When drawing close up, remember that the human body is subject to the rules of perspective. The seated figure with the head thrown back has its hips, chest and shoulders all parallel, but my viewpoint of it made me realise that the parallel lines would have to obey the rules of perspective if my sketch was to look convincing.

Preparing to draw from a model

When drawing from life, there is always more than one person to consider — yourself *and* your model. Not only must both of you be physically comfortable, but at ease with each other. This is much easier when you are drawing in a group, for instance at a life class from a professional model; but if you have asked someone specifically to pose for you, make sure first of all that they are relaxed. Tell your model what pose you want and to move about freely to find the most comfortable position. Also make sure that the place is warm and draught-free. Seated or lying poses are the easiest for the model to assume. Play the radio, or tapes. Carrying on a conversation, however, will divert you from your drawing.

Place yourself in a convenient situation where you can see the model in a good light, and with light on your paper so that your working hand does not throw a shadow across it, and your drawing things close by. I like to draw at an upright easel whenever possible, on large sheets of paper. Otherwise I use a very large layout pad as it encourages me to draw 'big'. The human body is a living, moving object, not inanimate material, and I want my lines and forms to express that quality.

Backgrounds can be as important or unimportant as you like to make them, but keep them simple: a cloth or drape is quite sufficient to set off the figure. A chair's shape can enhance a pose, but it should have some form of its own and not be a soft, upholstered object which distracts from the rounded forms and curves of your model. Avoid dramatic and 'photogenic' poses and gestures when posing your model — most drawings of these end up like caricatures. When you have finished drawing show your model your work — life-drawing is a shared experience between the sitter and the artist.

2B Pencil 9
on Cartridge.

Drawing the female form

Although the head proportions to the body are the same in both male and female — that is, eight head depths to each figure — the differences are quite considerable. The female body is smaller, the shoulders narrower and hips wider. The female carries more subcutaneous fat (breasts, hips, buttocks) and the limbs are slenderer and more rounded. Articulation is more pronounced around the hips because of the wider pelvic bones so that the female form appears more sinuous.

When you draw the female form, think of the torso as being two tapering blocks, one from the shoulders to the waist, the other joining it at the waist from the hip joints. These two blocks articulate at the waist and are held together by the spine. This can be seen in the drawing of the back of the nude on page 11.

When you draw from life, whatever your subject, try to rule out any preconceptions of what you think your drawing ought to look like. This will prevent you from glamorising your female studies. Accuracy in putting down what you see in front of you is the criterion for any objective drawing.

When I start to draw from the model I usually make a few rough sketches to get the 'feel' of the pose. As my pencil, pen or brush goes over the paper I am feeling outline, contour, mass. That is why in many of the drawings in this book you can see where I have made several attempts to find the correct line. I always leave these construction lines in for two reasons: first, the model may move slightly before I have finished drawing and such lines help me to correct the pose; and second, I feel that they actually add to the description of my subject. Drawing is a fluid art and anything that properly describes that attribute has a place in my studies.

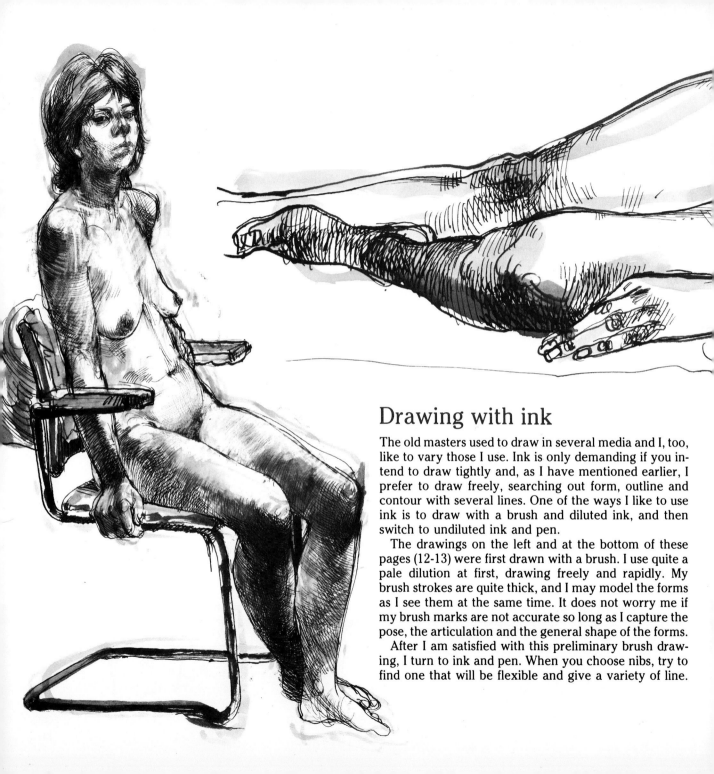

Drawing with ink

The old masters used to draw in several media and I, too, like to vary those I use. Ink is only demanding if you intend to draw tightly and, as I have mentioned earlier, I prefer to draw freely, searching out form, outline and contour with several lines. One of the ways I like to use ink is to draw with a brush and diluted ink, and then switch to undiluted ink and pen.

The drawings on the left and at the bottom of these pages (12-13) were first drawn with a brush. I use quite a pale dilution at first, drawing freely and rapidly. My brush strokes are quite thick, and I may model the forms as I see them at the same time. It does not worry me if my brush marks are not accurate so long as I capture the pose, the articulation and the general shape of the forms.

After I am satisfied with this preliminary brush drawing, I turn to ink and pen. When you choose nibs, try to find one that will be flexible and give a variety of line.

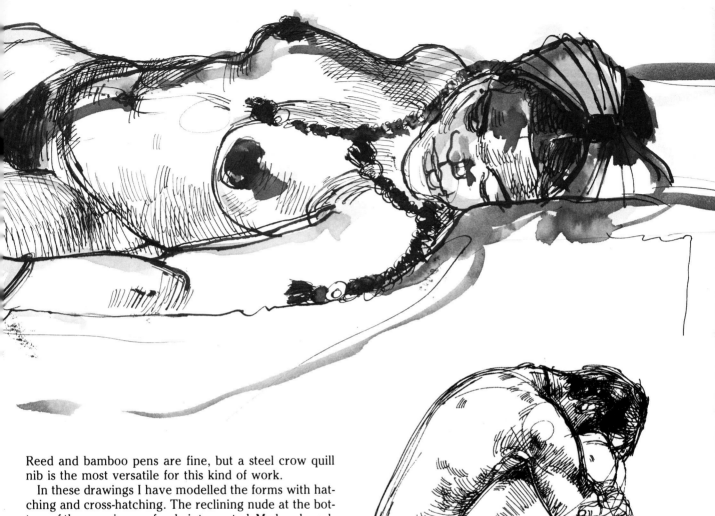

Reed and bamboo pens are fine, but a steel crow quill nib is the most versatile for this kind of work.

In these drawings I have modelled the forms with hatching and cross-hatching. The reclining nude at the bottom of the page is very freely interpreted. My brushwork and nib drawing is loose and uninhibited, yet the languor of the model is quite successfully portrayed. Pen and ink work is direct and vibrant and carries more force than pencil work.

On the right of page 13, I have drawn a crouching man in black ink with a crow quill pen. What interested me here was the overlapping forms of the arms and hands holding the knees tightly. Here you can see my construction lines quite clearly. Simple, tonal shading gives the sense of how the forms of torso, legs and arms are placed. Such a pose cannot be held for very long by the model, so I had to work quite quickly.

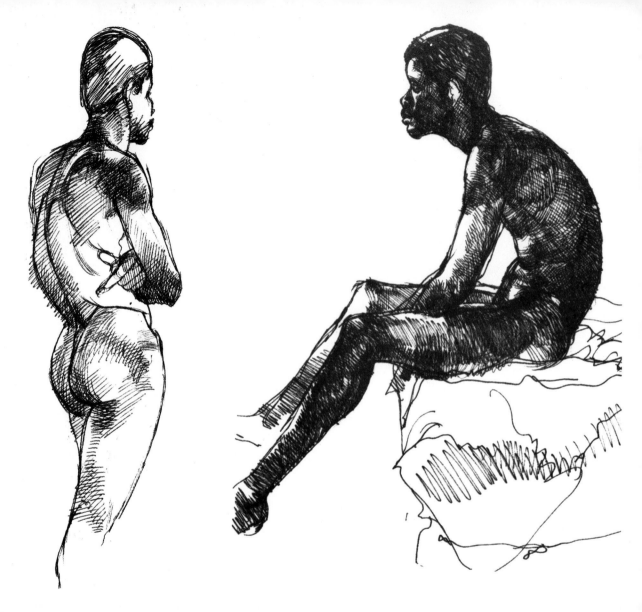

Skin tones

These two drawings of a black male model show not only carefully modelled form but also how local colour (his
black skin) can be expressed. In this case the shading on
the figure is 'pushed' to the darker end of the tonal spec-
trum so that the only white paper showing is on the
highlights.

Opposite is a page from my sketchbook. Drawn in pencil, the modelling of the forms is expressed by shading
which is then rubbed with the finger to resemble the
softness of the female skin.

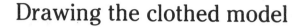

Drawing the clothed model

If you have been fortunate enough to draw and practise from a nude model, you will have some understanding of the human form and how it behaves in its various articulations. Drawing the clothed model need present no difficulties provided you understand what is going on underneath the clothes, and also how material drapes. A good exercise in understanding how clothes behave on the human form is to drape a piece of material, a curtain or a tablecloth, over an upright chair. Do not arrange it — just throw it over and see how the material touches the supporting parts, and how it folds and drapes away from it where it stands free of the support.

Clothes are designed to fit or drape — or both — over the human body. In the drawings opposite (page 17) I have indicated with arrows how, by the movements of the body, clothing is pulled against the underlying forms, and also the folds and creases caused by movements of the limbs. Sleeves and trousers are cylinders of cloth over cylindrical limbs. When the limbs move, the cloth surrounding them crumples and tautens, taking on its own shape, yet reflecting and echoing the forms underneath. Obvious stress points are where the cloth hangs from the body; the shoulders, or the knees when sitting. Other places are the breasts in women, elbows, wrists. Look for the places where the outline of the body changes direction — from these points the clothing covering them will fold, crease or straighten.

When drawing the clothed model always try to see the body underneath and look for the contact and stress points. Then your drawings will have conviction through their having understood the body beneath the clothes and your work will be more successful.

ing how clothing drapes
el to wear patterned or
and stripes will not only
ch you can follow the form,
y sudden changes in direction.
observantly, they provide useful
o follow with your drawing medium.
ning model (below) I have exaggerated
d the waistband of his pullover to show the changes of direction which describe the limbs and torso beneath. With the drawing of the standing girl on page 19 the stripes of her skirt change suddenly when the knee is bent and the leg changes direction. Look for such indications when you are drawing a clothed model.

Gesture drawing

Until now we have been considering the human body in repose. But one of the most exciting aspects of humans is their ability to present wonderful shapes and poses when going about some activity.

In many life classes the tutor will, during the session, ask the model to assume action poses. The model will then take up a stretching, bending, or other pose which suggests movement or action, and the class will be asked to draw quickly, for such poses can only be held for a short while. It is impossible to draw from such poses in a considered way, so what the tutor is asking of the students is to 'loosen up', to capture the 'feel' of the pose without faithful reference to the component parts and realistic shape of the posed body.

This is where gesture drawing comes into its own. Use the loosest technique that comes naturally to you: draw on large sheets of paper, and with a medium that is bold and expressive — a graphite stick, chalks or pastels. Feel straight away for the S-curve of the body, feel the pose inside yourself, and express it with movements of your drawing hand, and what you see before you.

These drawings were done in less than five minutes — the model could not hold out longer. Detail is ignored — what I was aiming to capture was the sense of extension and compression that the human body feels in these two poses. Gravity pulls at the body when it bends — notice how the breasts of the bending model are pulled by gravity away from the rib cage. The muscles of the model's legs in the crouching body are compressed.

Such gesture drawing studies are wonderful exercise for liberating techniques that have become too tight, and for understanding the versatility of the human body.

Foreshortening

As with all three-dimensional objects, the human body is subject to the rules of perspective. On page 7 you could see how perspective influences parallel lines. When you draw the body from close up, remember that those parts closest to you obey the rules of perspective and will appear bigger in proportion to those furthest away from you. The study on page 22 shows how I have drawn the knees and lower legs larger to emphasise how close to the model I was when I was drawing her.

Bodies in motion

Once you have learned how to represent the human form with sufficient confidence, try drawing people in motion.

I drew these footballers in action while I was watching television. I hardly lifted my pen from the paper and I probably only glanced at what I was actually doing a few times. Fortunately the human body repeats its shapes when in action, and I was able to build up the figures from observing several players at different times during the game. The trick here is to hold your eye on the subject, and not keep looking at what you are drawing.

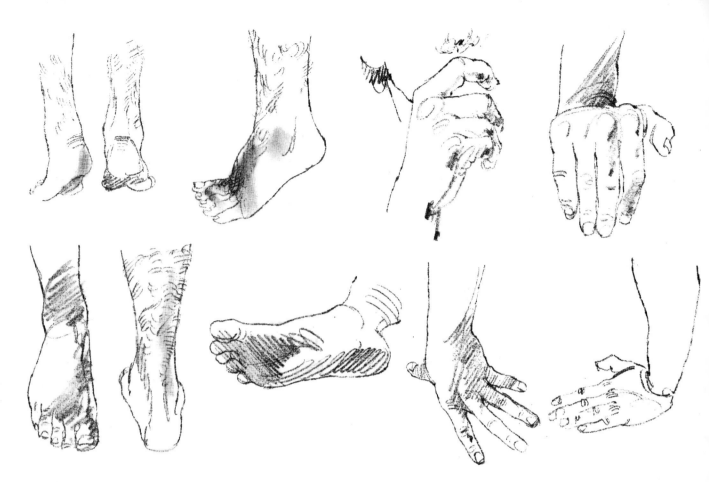

Extremities

Just as the head is a component of the body, so are hands and feet. Like the head, they are indicators of function and character. Some feet are broad, with well flexed toes — others are pinched and cramped by bad footwear. The hands can be calloused, cracked and rough-skinned, or soft and smooth and dainty according to the sex and occupation of your model.

Hands too are one of the ways in which people communicate meaning: they stop and beckon, scratch and pick, wave about when people are talking or shouting; they carry, hold and support. Make studies of hands and feet to understand how they work.

If you have nothing else to draw, you can always use your non-drawing hand as a model!

Drawing portraits

Drawing portraits is challenging and exacting. Not only do you have to satisfy your own artistic skills and judgement regarding your sitter, but also your sitter's opinion of what you have drawn. When drawing portraits you are tackling two things at once: an object — the head — which must also meet the criterion of being a likeness.

As a shape or form, the head can be thought of as an egg, with the point representing the chin. The height of the head, from chin to top, is one and a half times the distance between the cheeks. If you find difficulty in drawing the correct egg shape, draw a circle (or sphere) and then add the chin to this circle. Always try to see the *volume* of the head: then you can add the features — eyes, nose, mouth and ears — more easily to it.

Head proportions

These are simple guidelines to help you construct the features on a head (or 'egg'). They will, of course, vary slightly from sitter to sitter. The top row of head shapes shows our head in full face, three-quarter face and profile. The parallel lines show the divisions along which the features generally lie.

First, the head is divided into two equal sized parts. Along this line is placed the top of the ears and the eye line. This lower half is divided into two equal parts, and on the dividing line the bottom of the nose is placed. Divide this lower part similarly, and the bisecting line indicates where the mouth is placed. Notice that the depth of the nose corresponds to that of the ear.

Features

Once you have learned where the features are situated on or in the head, practise drawing them on their own. Sometimes drawing the eyes presents problems to the beginner, for they are recessed into the skull in their sockets, yet they also protrude slightly beyond the surface of the face. This protrusion is best seen when the head is tilted upwards; the eyelids follow the contours of the eyeballs.

Noses come in all shapes and sizes but, generally speaking, they are wedge-shaped, with the nostrils forming two small hemispheres on either side of the base. The mouth is the most expressive part of the face, regarding its ability to change its shape, and it also has a different texture and a more complex formation. In fact it is formed of two shapes, the upper and the lower lips. To understand its shapes I have drawn a diagrammatic mouth at the top left of this page. In order to define the shape of the mouth more clearly, draw in the fine striations of the lips, which follow the contours.

Ears can protrude at an angle from the head or be flattened against it. Their twists and turns can be difficult to draw and it is best to think of the ear's main shape as a block or wedge. Draw it lightly as such, then 'carve out' its component shapes and curves as you draw it in.

Below. *The head, although loosely sketched, bears out the underlying principles of drawing features: the wedge of the nose, the orbs of the eyes set in the skull, the striations on the lips defining their shape.*

Age extremes

From birth to maturity the shape of the skull is changing, and so altering the relationship of the feature. With on-coming old age the face shape will change as muscle tone lessens, eyesight becomes less sharp and dentistry alters the underlying configuration of the jaws.

Hair

Many students attempt to draw every lock and wisp of hair, and the results look indecisive and finicky. See hair rather as *masses* of form lying around and away from the head. By all means indicate the direction the hair falls or waves by some contour drawing, but the main aim is to indicate its mass in relationship to the head. The drawings on page 29 show different types of hair, but they also describe the shape of the skull underneath.

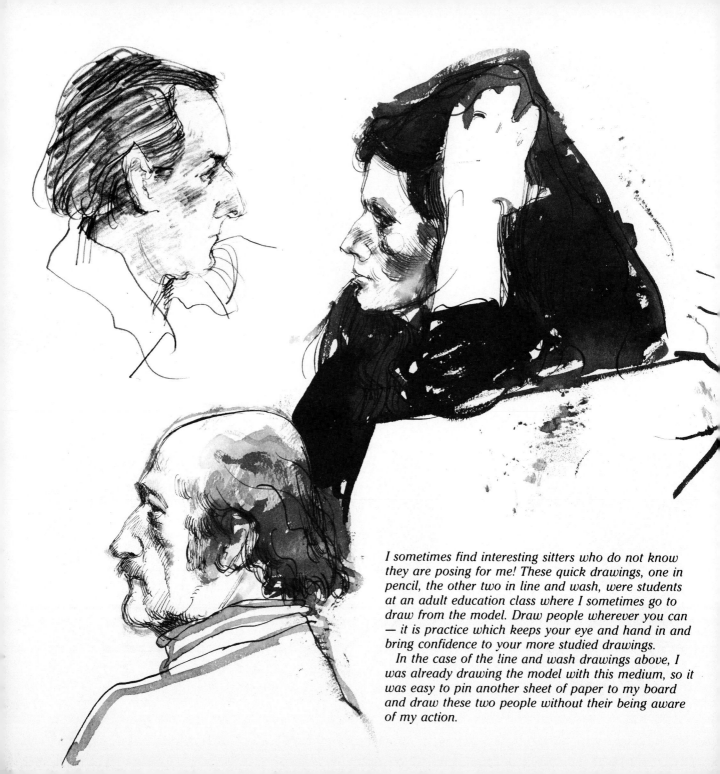

I sometimes find interesting sitters who do not know they are posing for me! These quick drawings, one in pencil, the other two in line and wash, were students at an adult education class where I sometimes go to draw from the model. Draw people wherever you can — it is practice which keeps your eye and hand in and bring confidence to your more studied drawings.

In the case of the line and wash drawings above, I was already drawing the model with this medium, so it was easy to pin another sheet of paper to my board and draw these two people without their being aware of my action.

Character and caricature

In order to emphasise character, I sometimes ask my sitters to wear clothes that are not their own. This helps me to create a character that is, maybe, at variance with the sitter's own personality, but I am aiming at a theatrical effect. Getting a sitter to pose with a glass in hand, wearing a special hat and scarf or, like the old lady above, holding a fan, gives my drawing an added element which, in her case, was in keeping with her character and at the same time produced a vivid drawing.

Sometimes I want to express an aspect of a person by exaggerating his or her features to the extent that the drawing resembles a caricature. Caricature is not easy — it is more a blend of exaggerated parts than singling out one salient feature and enlarging it. The two sketches on the right were done very swiftly — they are hardly likenesses, yet by concentrating on their hair, eyes and spectacles these two sketches border on caricatures of my sitters.

First published 1986
by Search Press Limited
Wellwood, North Farm Road
Tunbridge Wells, Kent, TN2 3DR

Text and illustrations by GEORGE CAYFORD

Reprinted 1987, 1989, 1991

Material from this volume, text and illustrations, has
previously been published in *Drawing for Pleasure*
(1983), edited by Peter D. Johnson and published
jointly by Search Press Ltd and Pan Books Ltd.

U.S. Artists Materials Trade Distributor:
Winsor & Newton, Inc.
P. O. Box 1519, 555 Winsor Drive, Secaucus, NJ07094

Canadian Distributors:
Anthes Universal Limited
341 Heart Lake Road South, Brampton,
Ontario L6W 3K8

Australian Distributors:
Jasco Pty. Limited
937-941 Victoria Road, West Ryde,
N.S.W. 2114

New Zealand Distributors:
Caldwell Wholesale Ltd
Wellington and Auckland

ISBN 085532 572 0

Typeset by Sprint
Printed in Spain by
Artes Graphicas Elkar, S. Coop.
Autonomía, 71 - 48012-Bilbao - Spain.

*Gesture drawings of two nudes.
The forms of the body are indicated
as much with the weight of line as
by the block shading.*